God loves even me

written and illustrated
by Debby Anderson

For Gordon, a loving dad

I want to thank You, God.

When I am sick, knowing You love me helps
me to feel better.

When I am sad and lonely, knowing You love me helps me to smile.

Knowing You love me makes me want to fly

like a bird.

God, You are always good ... but I'm not.

Sometimes I do bad things.

Thank You for patiently loving me.

And Lord please help me to patiently love, too.

"**F**or high as the heavens are above the earth, so great is His lovingkindness toward those who revere Him" (Psalm 103:11).

Just like a kind father, You always love me.

Lord, You know it is hard for me to be good
. . .

. . . **B**ut You love me even as I try.

Lord, Your kingdom rules over all. And

everyone everywhere

should thank You for Your love . . .

. . . **I** want to thank You, God, for Your love.

Psalm 103

Praise the Lord, O my soul;
  all my inmost being, praise his holy
    name.
Praise the Lord, O my soul,
  and forget not all his benefits.
He forgives all my sins
  and heals all my diseases;
He redeems my life from the pit
  and crowns me with love and
    compassion.
He satisfies my desires with good
    things,
  so that my youth is renewed like the
    eagle's.
The Lord works righteousness
  and justice for all the oppressed.
He made known his ways to Moses,
  his deeds to the people of Israel:
the Lord is compassionate and
    gracious,
  slow to anger, abounding in love.
He will not always accuse,
  nor will he harbor his anger forever;
he does not treat us as our sins deserve
  or repay us according to our
    iniquities.
For as high as the heavens are above
    the earth,
  so great is his love for those who fear
    him;

as far as the east is from the west,
  so far has he removed our
    transgressions from us.
As a father has compassion on his children,
  so the Lord has compassion on those
    who fear him;
for he knows how we are formed,
  he remembers that we are dust.
As for man, his days are like grass,
    he flourishes like a flower of the field;
the wind blows over it and it is gone,
  and its place remembers it no more.
But from everlasting to everlasting
  the Lord's love is with those who
    fear him,
  and his righteousness with their
    children's children—
with those who keep his covenant
  and remember to obey his precepts.
The Lord has established his throne in
    heaven,
  and his kingdom rules over all.
Praise the Lord, you his angels,
  you mighty ones who do his bidding,
  who obey his word.
Praise the Lord, all his heavenly hosts,
  you his servants who do his will.
Praise the Lord, all his works
  everywhere in his dominion.
Praise the Lord, O my soul.

Scripture Text: *The Holy Bible, New International Version* © 1978 by New York International Bible Society.
Used by permission of New York International Bible Society